Birth Stories
of the
Prophets

Birth Stories
of the
Prophets

Dede Khan

Illustrated by
Henriette Willebeek le Mair

East-West Publications London and the Hague

All enquiries to:- East-West Publications (U.K.) Ltd.,
115–123 Bayham Street, London NW1 0AL.

First published 1978

Illustrations © 1978 Soefi Stichting Inayat Fundatie Sirdar
Text © 1978 Dede Khan
Production and design services by Elron Press Ltd., London WC2.

ISBN 0 85692 021 5

Printed and bound in Great Britain by
Butler & Tanner Ltd.

Contents

1. Introduction   6

2. Krishna   11

3. Buddha   21

4. Zoroaster   33

5. Abraham   45

6. Jesus   57

7. Mohammed   69

1

Introduction

Religion is as old as mankind. Through the ages people have needed their faith to find answers to questions that were unanswerable, and to find strength in the knowledge that there is a God who understands all.

As there were, still are, and always will be many different people who are living in different countries, in different environments and under different circumstances, there have to be as many different ideas, and consequently, to suit the mentalities of all these widely differing people, different explanations of the one Message of God.

All these various ideas should be regarded as different roads, all of them leading to that one final point: the One and Only God.

From the very beginning it was necessary, especially in difficult times, that landmarks should be given to the people walking on those roads to show them the right paths. These landmarks sent by God were the Prophets. And the Prophets came down to the Earth to guide the people, and their actions and teachings had to be adapted to the environments and the circumstances of that particular country they were sent to, at that particular period they were placed in.

It should be far from us to say of one Prophet that he is greater than another, or to have a prejudice against some ideas because their ways and means might look different from the ways and means that we are used to; we might only say that the teachings of one particular Prophet are clearer to us than the teachings of another Prophet, or that one particular belief appeals to us more than another.

The intention with which this book has been prepared is to make children all over the world become acquainted with the fact that there have been many Prophets. Their birth stories as told here are like fairy tales and have been selected for children as they are easy to read and easy to understand.

Let us try to see the Prophets as landmarks sent out to groups of people who were confused, not knowing which road to take; let us try to remember gratefully their teachings; and let us try to realise that, no matter what their habits might have been, or where they lived, they were sent to this Earth to help mankind find the road to the One and Only God.

Krishna

2

Krishna

This story is old, ages old; it took place in India, in the lands of Braj, a country which is situated on the banks of the Yamuna river, a sacred river, known to all Hindus.

There lived a king at that time and his name was Kansa. Due to his actions it was said that he was the son of a demon, and although his parents had been faithful and good people who had tried to educate him according to their religion and their standards, they had not been able to prevent their son from committing one crime after another. And the time came when the boy grew up and became a man and when, aided by his armed forces, he had dethroned his father who had been a good king all his life.

Kansa was not a good king; he dreamed of more power and he was ruthless in his actions to achieve greater splendour and greater wealth. He led his armies into many battles and always the victories were his. Many countries were conquered and the time came when Kansa was called the universal ruler of the lands of Braj. The rich and the powerful joined their king and followed him in this ceaseless longing for more wealth, and no one ever thought of the poor who became even poorer and more miserable during his reign.

God saw it all. He saw the material welfare of the rich living in their wealthy palaces; He looked into their hearts and He saw that they were no longer concerned about Him or His Commandments. God also saw the starving poor, leading their miserable lives in their small cheap huts, wondering how to obtain food for the next day. And God in His great wisdom decided that the time had come for Him to send a Prophet to the Earth. And from His great height,

God looked down on the people and He selected two young persons who would be the parents of this child who was to become His Prophet: a descendant of King Brajman of the old noble Yadu family would be the father, his name was Vasudeva; and the mother would be Devaki, a young, faithful and religious niece of King Kansa. And God made love enter their hearts and they fell in love with each other and they were to be married.

On that day when the wedding ceremony was to be performed, there was much joy and splendour in the lands of Braj and the people came out of their houses in beautiful clothes and they rejoiced.

In those days it was a custom at important marriages that the king would lead the wedding procession through the city, and so it happened that King Kansa was leading the procession on the occasion of the marriage of Devaki and Vasudeva. But when the magnificent procession entered the city of Mathura, the capital of Braj, Kansa, in the middle of all the splendour and joy, suddenly heard an unknown voice coming down from the Heavens, and the voice was stern and spoke: "Oh, Kansa, the eighth child of your niece, whose wedding procession you are leading now, will be a son and he will be the cause of your losing your power, and you will die by his hand."

And Kansa, aghast, fear gripping him suddenly in its deadly power, turned to Devaki in an outburst of anger, and would have killed her at that very instant, if Vasudeva had not thrown himself at the king's feet, begging him to spare her and promising that every child that would be born to them, would be given to Kansa. These words seemed to have their influence: Kansa came to his senses again and he agreed to this proposal.

And so it happened during the years that went by, that joy and happiness disappeared from the lives of Vasudeva and Devaki. Every child born to them had to be brought to Kansa who would have it killed immediately. Seven sons were born and seven sons were killed.

But still the king did not feel safe. Fear had entered his heart years ago when he had heard the stern voice coming down from the Heavens, prophesying his death, and this fear did not leave him day or night. And thinking of all the possible means to secure his worldly power, he had himself surrounded by his ministers and asked them what more he could do to be sure that no one would kill him. And the old advisers looked at their king who during these years had grown old due to his constant worry and fear, and they shook their heads and fingered their beards and they advised him to have every descendant of the Yadu family killed, thinking that only then their king might find peace.

And soldiers were sent out into the country, to the towns, the villages and the houses, and they killed every man and woman and child they could find who belonged to the family of Yadu. Despair and sorrow swept the country. Many people fled and left their homes to find peace in other places. And every descendant of the Yadu family who was not killed, tried to cross the Yamuna river to reach the shepherd village of Gokul where they were received with open arms by Nanda, the chief of the shepherds who was a great friend of Vasudeva.

During this time, when despair and death in the form of murdering soldiers ruled the lands of Braj, Devaki was expecting her eighth child. Kansa, being haunted day and night by the image of this child who was to kill him one day, had her thrown into prison together with Vasudeva and he had the prison surrounded by elephants, lions, wild dogs and armed soldiers.

And so the stage was properly set for the birth of a Prophet of God.

It happened on a Friday night, at midnight. Devaki woke up in prison feeling that her time to have her child had come. She woke up Vasudeva to tell him, and at that very instant it suddenly seemed as if the ceiling of their cell had become transparent. A strange and beautiful light seemed to come down from the Heavens, and before their astonished eyes there appeared the vision of the child she was going to have. It seemed as if he was standing on air, and his body had a deep blue shiny colour like the endless blue beauty of the sky; his face showed the quiet silver white light of the moon; his eyes looked like open lotus flowers; around his waist there was a silken yellow sash; a crown was placed on his head, and around his neck there glittered a necklace with many beautiful precious stones.

The parents looked at this beautiful child. They wanted to utter a prayer but were speechless, knowing that God had come to them, and in God's presence there should only be silence.

Then the vision spoke and said: "I am to be your son, but after I am born, you, Vasudeva, will have to bring me to Gokul where a girl has just been born to Nanda and his wife Yasoda. And I will stay with them for some time, but I will return to you after I have killed King Kansa."

After these words the vision disappeared, the light in the cell became dim again and a son was born to Devaki. His name was Krishna. And all along the banks of the Yamuna river and far out into the world this name would be known and respected through the ages.

But Vasudeva and Devaki could not know this yet. Their only immediate concern was how to prevent this son from falling into Kansa's hands. And while they were thinking of this, God made it clear to them in His special way: suddenly Vasudeva felt the iron shackles with which he had been tied to the wall, fall from his wrists and feet. Devaki looked at him and was astonished to see him being able to move about, and they could not believe their eyes when they saw the doors of the prison being quietly opened as if by invisible hands, and they saw the guards outside lying down in a deep and heavy sleep. Vasudeva picked up the child, wrapped some cloth around it and put it in a basket usually used for grain, and he put the basket on his head. Then he walked out of the prison and no one seemed to notice and no one barred his way. And God made heavy rain pour down from the sky so as to wash away his footprints. He heard the roaring of the lions behind them but they did not come near. He walked to the banks of the Yamuna, and as he was near, the water suddenly stopped its forceful flow and made way for him. It was all like a dream to him. He went through the river, carefully carrying the basket with the slumbering child, and came to Gokul. And when they arrived at the house of Nanda, he found the doors open and everyone in a deep sleep. He found the cradle with the little baby girl and he took her out and put Krishna in her place. Then he put the girl in the basket and returned to the prison with her along the same way as he had come. Behind them the Yamuna river started flowing again, the prison doors closed again and the heavy irons tied themselves around his wrists and feet.

The guards, on hearing the cries of the baby, woke up, the noise of their weapons making the lions roar louder and angrier.

At that moment when the night was pitch black, when the earth was trembling under the heavy rains and thunderstorm, Kansa woke up in his golden palace and heard the voice of his memory again, the voice that he feared: "Great king, your enemy is born."

Furiously in his fear and anger, he hurried to the prison where he snatched the little baby from Devaki's arms, and seeing that it was a girl and not a boy as he had thought it would be, he lifted her up to kill her immediately, but God made her escape from his angry hands, and she disappeared and was never heard of again.

With renewed energy, an energy fed by fear and by anger, Kansa again tried to get hold of all children belonging to the Yadu family so as to kill this one descendant that he feared so much.

It was by his orders that the female monster called Putana went about killing the children in the lands of Braj. On her way she also entered Gokul and as she assumed the form of a most beautiful and lovely woman no one stopped her. She moved about freely in the village and at last entered the house of Nanda. She looked like a kind mother and Yasoda liked her looks so much that she did not stop her going to Krishna's cradle and taking him out. Then Putana put the child on her lap and gave him milk full of a deadly poison from her breast. Krishna at once felt who this woman was and what her intentions were. He held on to her breast with both hands and angrily drank and drank and went on drinking in the very life juice of the woman. She felt his anger, she understood his power and she screamed for help that someone would take this child away. Casting up and down her hands and feet, she slowly felt life go from her and at last she fell dead. At the same moment she lost the looks of the beautiful woman and became a monster again. Yasoda hearing all the noise, ran in and became very frightened seeing the dead monster. She took the child and washing it, prayed over it and cared for it. By this time Nanda returned home. Seeing the huge body of the monster he once more realised the extent of Kansa's hate.

That evening the monster's body was burned and the smoke rising into the air was sweet-scented: only the touch of Krishna's body purified even the enemy.

With growing childhood Krishna became very naughty, and the women of the village often came to Yasoda to complain as he would untie the cows before milking time, or he would steal milk and curds and quietly sit down in a corner and eat as much as he wanted. Then he used to go to the monkeys who were always around and divide whatever was left. If he did not find something to eat, he would break the pots. If the pots were out of reach he would, by climbing on seats or stools, find some way to reach them. And when the women got angry he would betray his guilt by the fear in his eyes. But Yasoda never beat him, she only smiled.

One day some boys from the neighbourhood came to Yasoda to tell her that Krishna had been a dirty boy and eaten earth. Yasoda was rather upset and told him to open his mouth so that she could examine it. When she looked into it, something wonderful happened: she was no longer examining the mouth of a child, but she was looking into the beauty of the whole universe. She saw the planets and the stars, the earth and the moon, she even saw herself placed in all this, in the middle of the glittering of the stars, the flowing rivers of the Earth and the quiet valleys of the moon. She sent Krishna away to play again and she stayed alone in the house thinking of the immense power of this child.

Another day it happened that Yasoda was churning curdled milk and singing. Krishna came in and helped her, holding the churning rod. Then she gave him some milk to drink. But the milk that was boiling on the oven overflowed and she hurriedly left him. Angry at being left alone Krishna bit his lips, broke the milk pot with a stone and after taking some fresh butter, left the house. After a while Yasoda came back and seeing the broken pot she understood that Krishna had been busy. She went out and found him sitting on the lawn, eating some butter himself and dividing the rest among the monkeys who would come near, snatch some butter from him and then run off into the trees. Yasoda got hold of him and being rather angry, tried to fasten him to the husking stand, but the rope fell short by two fingers. She took another rope and added it to the first one, but the gap remained the same. She added rope after rope but could not bridge the gap. Amazed and realising that she could

not tie this child up, she stepped back. Then Krishna, seeing her tiredness, allowed himself to be fastened to the stand.

And God's blessing was on the village and its people. In those years
it seemed as if the flowers wanted to be more beautiful than ever,
their colours showing wonderful patterns, and their fragrance filling
the air. The leaves of the trees gave more shadow during the heat
than before and the fruits growing in between the leaves were full
and heavy. The rivers and the mountain streams showed the weeds
growing in their depths as the water was so pure and clear that it
seemed like waves of dancing crystal. The birds whistled happy
tunes, and the people in the village saw it all and wondered what
had happened to nature. The word 'sorrow' became unknown in
those days when Krishna grew up among shepherds in the small village of Gokul, on the other side of the river.

Ages have passed. The name of Kansa might have been forgotten
and if it is still remembered it is only because he was a cruel ruler
who vainly tried to kill a Prophet of God. But all along the banks
of the Yamuna river, faithful people will come together to say their
prayers and they will remember the man who, although born in a
prison, carried within him God's promise for a better world, and
who, on leaving this Earth, left mankind his books full of wisdom
as an eternal evidence of his prophethood.

Buddha

3

Buddha

Long, long ago, the Soul whose Essence is Wisdom, dwelled in the Heavens. His name was Bodhisattva and he was perfect. A million stars, moving about in the skies like glittering jewels, observed his perfection and they whispered about it for twelve years. Then they decided to approach the God of Gods and ask Him whether the Bodhisattva could be sent down to the Earth in the form of a human being to become the Buddha, God's Prophet, and spread the eternal wisdom amongst the peoples on the ten horizons of the Earth.

After receiving this request, God turned his attention to Bodhisattva and seeing the enlightenment and the inner wisdom of his soul, God knew that he would be capable of becoming the Buddha. But before taking a decision, God wished to make what are called the five great observations concerning the time, the continent, the country, the family and the mother of the future Buddha.

And God saw the people on the Earth who were lost in their daily struggles and who desperately needed an enlightened soul among them to lead them on to the road of righteousness. And in His great love for mankind God decided that the right time had come. It was 563 B.C.

Looking over the four continents of the world surrounded by isles and seas, God reflected that in the fourth continent, and specifically in the subcontinent of India, the Buddha should be born. And thus, in His great wisdom, God decided on the continent.

Next came the observation concerning the country. Seeing that

India was immensely large, the God of Gods decided that the future Buddha should be born near the town of Kapilavasthu in a country which is now called Nepal, at the foot of the Himalayas.

The observation regarding the family was that the future Buddha should be born into a warrior family, highclass so that his teachings could reach far. Thus God's decision fell on the Sakya clan as they had a reputation for their pride and piety. Although originally of the warrior caste, they cultivated the peaceful art of agriculture.

Then God, from His great height, saw the last descendant of the Sakya clan, King Suddhodana and his wife, Queen Maha Maya, both of whom were pious, following the teachings of the faith. And thus God made his last decision that they would be the parents of the future Buddha.

And the God of Gods in the Heavens above, summoned Bodhisattva to His side and He called the stars to inform them that His five great decisions had been made, and that the time had come for Bodhisattva to be reborn on Earth as Siddhartha Gautama, son of King Suddhodana and Queen Maha Maya.

It seemed as if, after this decision, the stars glittered more profoundly and more beautifully than ever.

It is related that during those days the Midsummer Festival had been proclaimed six days previous to the day of the full moon and in Kapilavasthu the people, dressed in lovely bright colours, were enjoying the festivities together with King Suddhodana and Queen Maha Maya.

On the evening of the full moon, the queen, tired from all the festivities, bathed in perfumed water and dressed herself beautifully, after which she retired to the elegantly furnished Chamber of State and fell asleep, dreaming the following dream:

From the sky there descended four guardian angels who lifted her up and took her away to the Himalayan Mountains. There they withdrew, and other angels came and brought her to Anotatta Lake, where they carefully bathed her as if to remove every human stain from her body. They clothed her in divine garments, and decked her with heavenly flowers. Then they brought her to the Golden Mansion on Silver Hill where they spread a divine couch for her. While resting there a new feeling of happiness and peace slowly came over her and she could relax as never before.

Her dream continued and to her astonished eyes there appeared a beautiful white elephant who came towards the couch on which she was resting. In his silvery trunk he brought her a white lotus which he carefully and with reverence put at her feet. Then he trumpeted loudly and to her it seemed as if he wanted to announce a message, so far unknown, to the world. Three times this beautiful animal circled round her couch, lightly touching her with his trunk. With his last touch she woke up and saw that she was lying in the Chamber of State of the Palace. There was no white elephant to be seen, but at her feet lay the beauty of one single white lotus flower.

She got up and told her husband about this strange and wonderful dream. Next day he summoned sixty-four Brahmans, eminent wise religious men. He gave them costly food, sweets and drinks, and after they had eaten and drunk, he told them the queen's dream. With every word that he uttered it seemed as if the Brahmans became more intent, and when he came to the end of the story, the oldest of the wise men got up, tears of happiness shone in his eyes, and with a great joy in his voice he said:

"Be not anxious, Oh Great King; you will become the father of a person whose coming has been predicted in many Holy Books. He has been appointed by God to make a most important choice when he comes of age; a choice which will have its reflection on

mankind. If your son continues to lead a normal life in your household, he will grow up to become a Universal Monarch, respected
and loved by all. But if he leaves the normal household life you can
offer him, and retires from the world, then he will become the
Buddha, God's Prophet; he will set an example by his great compassion for the sufferers and the needy on this earth, and animals will
come to him and be grateful for his loving touch. He will come to
remove the veil of ignorance and folly from this world, and God's
blessings and love will be with him for always."

The king had been listening in astonishment, and when the Brahmans had left, he went to the queen and told her what the old wise
man had said. And only then did he notice the strange golden light
which seemed to be shining from within the queen and which
strongly illuminated the whole palace and the gardens. With happiness and gratitude in their hearts they thanked God for this wonder
which was to take place in their lives. And, as if in answer to their
prayer, they saw four angels with swords in their hands who
would keep guard to ward off all harm from the future Buddha's
mother.

And it is told that, from the moment that the future Buddha was
known to be born, many miracles took, place in the large subcontinent of India:

An unknown light illuminated the whole Universe from horizon
to horizon; the blind, as if eager to see the beauty of Bodhisattva,
got back their sight; the deaf, anxious to hear his speech, could hear
again; the mute, as if given the ability to speak of him, recovered
their speech; the hunch-backs suddenly became straight normal
people; the lame could walk over the earth again; the fire of hell
was extinguished; hunger, thirst and illnesses ceased to exist; and
animals stopped being afraid of people.

It seemed as if even nature and the characters of people changed:

the hateful became friendly, the jealous became full of joy at other people's prosperity and the selfish became generous. During the days and the nights of the warm season there was a cool breeze and refreshing rains fell during the warmest days of the year. The waters of the seas became sweet and were covered by waterlilies. And musical instruments sent the most lovely music into the air without anyone having touched them.

Really and truly, the whole of the Universe was joyfully preparing itself to receive this child, this son of King Suddhodana and Queen Maha Maya, who was to become the Buddha, a teacher for all ages to come.

When the queen felt that her time had come, she wanted to go home to Devadaha where her relatives lived. The king, approving of this as she had not seen her people for a long time, made all arrangements for her journey himself, making certain that she would be comfortable. With the king's strongest horses and biggest elephants, it became a most beautiful procession.

In between Kapilavasthu and Devadaha lies a pleasure grove of saltrees called Lumbini Grove. It used to be a beautiful garden, but during this particular season it really seemed as if the greatest of nature's miracles had taken place there: all trees were blossoming and the grove was one mass of wonderful coloured flowers from the ground to the topmost branches; roses were growing on hard, grey, immovable rocks and all over the garden there was the play and spell of light and shadow. There were so many gay and happy colours around that it seemed as if it was raining flowers from the skies. The bees were humming contentedly and the birds whistled their happy songs from early morning until late at night.

When the queen's procession passed through this garden, she wanted to walk among the flowers and the trees to enjoy the colours and happiness around her. But suddenly she felt that her baby was coming and maid servants came quickly to hang sheets around her. It was there, in Lumbini Grove, while the queen was standing and holding on to a branch of one of the saltrees, surrounded by nature's beauty, that the future Buddha was born.

Four angels carrying a golden net, came down from the Heavens to receive the baby boy and when they carefully wanted to place him on the ground, there suddenly sprouted and unfolded a beautiful pure white lotus whose petals seemed to be eager to enfold the baby, and so the angels placed the child on the heavy strong, silken white leaves. The queen, looking at this pure and lovable child, felt her eyes fill with tears of joy and gratitude. Then, with a soft rustling sound, two streams of water came from the sky to refresh the Buddha and his mother.

Great was the king's joy when he received the news from messengers. At once he left the palace and went out to Lumbini Grove where he was struck by the beauty nature displayed before him. He saw his son lying safely on the strong petals of the white lotus flower, he saw the streams of water coming down from a clear blue sky, and he remembered the words of the old Brahman: "But if he will leave the household life, he will become a Prophet and God's love will be with him for always." And the king's heart filled with a fresh feeling of reverence towards this newlyborn baby.

Then, with much splendour, he arranged the return journey to Kapilavasthu, and all along the roads of the country and the cities, wherever the procession passed, people stood outside their houses as throughout the country the news of the king's newly-born son, being an exceptionally wonderful lovable child, had been heard. And they threw flowers on the road and begged the king and queen to bring this child into their home for a moment only so that the house with all its inmates might be blessed.

Days passed quickly in this happy atmosphere of Kapilavasthu, and after some time—it must have been nearly a year later—the old custom of the "Sowing Festival", celebrated in the city and the lands around it on a certain day of the year, was to take place.

On that day the whole city used to be decorated, all the servants would be given new tunics and they would assemble together in front of the king's palace where a thousand ploughs were yoked.

The plough which was to be held by the king was ornamented with red gold, as also the horns, the reins and the goads for the oxen; one hundred and seven ploughs, to be used by the court attendants, were ornamented with silver, including the reins for the oxen and the cross bars of the ploughs; and the other, ordinary ploughs were to be handled by the farmers.

This time the king took his son with him, and when arriving in the field where the ploughing was to take place, the king had a couch placed in the dense shade of a solitary rose-apple tree. He placed the young prince on it and over his head he spread a canopy studded with golden stars. Nurses were appointed to keep watch over the baby boy.

Then the king took the golden plough, the court attendants took the silver ploughs, and the farmers took the other ones and they all went to the fields they were to plough.

The nurses sitting in the sun, chatting together and eating sweets, forgot to pay any attention to Bodhisattva, who quietly moved away from his magnificent couch and playfully crawled off, following the colours of the butterflies and the humming of the bees. When he was tired he sat down a little further on the grass and fell asleep.

Suddenly the nurses remembered that they had left their young master alone and when they saw his couch empty, they went to look for him. They found him asleep on the grass and to their great astonishment they noticed that the rose-apple tree seemed to be bent in such a way that the child was still in its shadow; although all the shadows of the other trees had passed over to the east, the shadow of this particular tree was bent over to the west.

The nurses saw the miracle and hurried to the king, who at once came back with them to witness this wonder of nature going out of its way to shield his son from the piercing sunbeams. And again the feeling of reverence touched his heart: "His son would be a Prophet."

A short while later, the king wished that his son should be brought to the temple. When this became known in the city, it was the request of the people that on that occasion the young prince should wear all the ornaments and jewels fit for the son of the king. But it happened that, at the moment these most beautiful jewels and silver and golden bracelets and necklaces touched the child, they became dark and lifeless and dead in comparison to the splendour which shone from the boy himself.

When the king carried him in his arms to the temple, surrounded by all the wise men from the court, the high officials, the priests and the people of the city, it seemed as if heavenly music moved through the atmosphere, and the beauty of the child was so wonderful to behold that for a long time to come the people in Kapilavasthu talked of this splendid day.

In those days it happened that a wise old man, named Asita, who lived on the side of the Himalayan Mountains and used to read the stars, saw a new great diamond appear in the sky, and every night it would be there again, glittering in many colours. Asita went out on foot in search of its meaning and when his road finally brought him into the city of King Suddhodana, where he heard the news of the birth of a beautiful son to the king and the exceptional things that had taken place since his birth, he decided to go to the palace.

The king, knowing that Asita was a wise and learned man, made him enter the Chamber of State and the servants washed his hands and feet. Then he had dishes with lovely food put in front of the old man so that he might satisfy his hunger and quench his thirst. And Asita gratefully accepted all the king's hospitality. When he was satisfied, he looked up and told the king that he had walked all the way from the side of the Himalayan Mountains in search of the meaning of the new diamond in the sky, and that, on arriving in Kapilavasthu he had heard of the birth of Siddhartha Gautama. And he respectfully requested the king to show him his son.

The king left the side of Asita to return after a short while with his child in his arms. The wise man, struck by the beauty of the boy, immediately recognised certain marks that had been predicted to be carried by the future Buddha, and, knowing that his search had ended, that the appearance of the new beautiful star was explained, and that he was face to face with the Prophet of God, he got up from his seated position and with joined hands did reverence to the child. Then he looked up and with a voice quivering from emotion, he spoke:

"Great King, your son will be the King of Laws; he will be the Master of the Empires; he will be great and many people will follow him. He has been chosen by God to be His Prophet. No human being will be equal to him and his name will be praised, his actions remembered and his teachings followed until the end of time."

And it was the third time that the king wanted to do reverence to his son.

Asita left the palace. On foot he returned to his house on the side of the Himalayan Mountains. His steps were slow. He was deep in thought. Realising that he would die before the time had come when the child would have become the Buddha, he knew that it would not be given to him ever to hear the teachings of the Prophet of God. And the old wise man Asita wept. His tears were noticed by the people that passed him. They asked him the reason and when he explained why he cried, they withdrew in silence, but in their hearts they carried his words and kept his tears as a living proof that Gautama, the young prince, who was born in Lumbini Grove, who lived in their midst and whose star shone in exceptional brightness, was to be the Buddha, who had come down from the Heavens to spread the eternal wisdom amongst the peoples on the ten horizons of the Earth.

Zoroaster

4

Zoroaster

His name was Zoroaster, the Blessed One, and it was said that he was born from the Light which is Endless. One particle from this Light fled away, on to the sun; and from the sun it was reflected and fled on to the moon; from the moon it fled on to the stars; and from the stars it was reflected and fled on to Earth.

His birth took place in a country which at that time was called Media, situated near Iran in Asia. When he became 30 years of age he went to Iran to live and preached there for the rest of his life, which is the reason why his name for all years and ages to come would be connected with Iran.

But all this is a long, long time ago and the country of Media cannot be found on any maps any more.

In those days, long ago, the situation in the whole country of Media was pitiful. There was confusion everywhere as the people in their thoughts and in their daily actions had moved far from the Word of God; His teachings and commandments had long been forgotten, and it seemed as if the people were imprisoned in the claws of the Devil, rejoicing in their bad, mean and unfaithful behaviour.

God, with His endless love for mankind, His most wonderful creation, felt His heart grow with compassion for their foolishness. In His great mercy He decided to send a Guide to Earth, a Prophet who would open the door to the people to show them again that the only way to attain real inner happiness was the road leading upwards to Him. And God looked around to find a family which would be worthy of raising His Prophet, and He saw the descendants of the family of Faridun. An ancient royal line, who notwithstanding the utter confusion and wickedness of the people around them, still tried to follow the right path, keeping to His commandments and saying their prayers. And God's search ended when he saw the youngest son of this family and his wife, called Purshasp and Doghduyah. Purshasp was a strong and honest man with a clear eye and Doghduyah was a dignified woman bearing herself with pride. And God smiled, knowing that His choice was good.

They were a happy couple and their happiness became complete when she learned that she was pregnant. Yet, they were quite ignorant of the fact that they had been chosen by God to fulfil His purpose. And to make them understand that their child was to be an outstanding person, God touched Doghduyah with the Light which is Endless at the very moment she first discovered that she was with child. And from that day onwards the Light shone within and around her.

Wherever she moved, the Light went with her so that, when she sat close to a fire, the flames would look dull in comparison to the radiance which shone from her being. The people of the city noticed it, and it was said that, when Doghduyah came to visit them in the evenings, it was not necessary to light the lamps as the Light she carried with her was strong enough to illuminate the house.

After about five and a half months of pregnancy, Doghduyah had a heavenly vision in a dream:

There was a large dark cloud which completely enveloped the house, shutting out the golden beams of the sun and the silver shine of the moon. And in her dream the cloud seemed to become bigger and bigger and then, all at once, it broke open and it rained wild beasts from the cloud: lions and tigers, crocodiles, panthers, wolves and many more animals. They came down like a frightening, angry rain with outstretched claws and open mouths. And then Doghduyah suddenly saw a child sitting in the midst of them all. It looked so small and innocent and even in her dream she knew that it was hers: the child she was expecting at the moment. And her heart screamed through fear when she saw one of the wild beasts wanting to throw himself on the child and tear it to pieces, but the little boy turned his head, looked at her, smiled a heavenly smile and said: "The good God is my friend, do not have any fears." And a great peaceful feeling came over Doghduyah.

Her dream continued: she saw a shining white mountain slowly come down from the Heavens and the dark cloud was destroyed by the fierce bright light. When the mountain in all its glaring beauty came nearer, a young man walked out of the light; he was dressed in shining white garments; in one hand he held a luminous branch and in the other hand the Book of God which, in a sudden gesture, he threw towards the wild animals and they fled in wild disorder; only a wolf, a lion and a tiger stayed. The youth came near and hit them with the luminous branch and to her astonishment Doghduyah saw them being consumed by the fire. Then the young man picked up the child which smiled happily and he said: "Have no fears, for God Himself, the Creator of the universe, is the guardian of your son and nothing bad will ever happen to him as long as he lives for he will be a Prophet of God." After these words the youth and the child slowly disappeared, the vision faded and Doghduyah woke up.

She trembled from head to foot and wished with all her heart that Purshasp were with her, but he had left on a trading journey a few days earlier. And although it was still the middle of the night she could no longer stay in the house but had to tell someone about this vision and ask for an explanation.

And so she went to an old wise man, a seer, who lived close by and she told him her dream. He looked at her for a very long time, first he seemed astonished and then gradually, he smiled respectfully at her and said:

"The appearance of your son in this world will be like the bright light of the sun after the darkness of night; in strength and in splendour there will be none equal to him and he will be greater than any other living being."

Then the old seer became silent and meditated for a long while. Doghduyah waited until the old man looked at her again, saying:

"His name will be Zoroaster, the Blessed One, and he will destroy all the enemies of the faith who will try to fight him in every possible way and you, oh, Doghduyah, shall have many fears for the life of your son, as you feared the wild beasts in your vision. But in the end you will find happiness and rejoice in Zoroaster's victories. The youth you saw in your dream carrying the glittering branch is the Angel Gabriel, the Splendour of God, who will shield your son from all evil. And the Book of God which was in his hand, is the Godly sign that your son will be a Prophet and that he will obtain victory over all evil.

"He will have three great enemies like the three wild animals that stayed after all the others fled away, and who in the end were consumed by the fire of the glittering branch. They will be the worst of mankind and they will try everything within their power to destroy your son Zoroaster. But finally he will be able, with the help of God, to destroy them. And the time will come that there shall be a God-fearing prince who will make Zoroaster sovereign of this world and the next. Paradise will be given to those who follow his commandments and the souls of his enemies will burn in the everlasting fires of hell."

Then the old seer suddenly closed his eyes, lifted his face up towards the Heavens and with tears of longing streaming down his wrinkled cheeks and grey beard, he prayed:

"Oh, that it would be granted to me to live during the coming years, so that I could devote my soul, my heart and my services to the Prophet Zoroaster."

Doghduyah had been listening to the explanations of this wise man with a mixture of growing astonishment, excitement and gratitude in her heart. Finally, with a trembling voice, she asked him how he knew all these things were to take place, and the old seer replied that it had been written in Holy Books and old scriptures that during this time a child would be born who would be a Prophet of God and that the stars had given him their message and the knowledge that the time was near.

After these words Doghduyah became silent and she went home and when her husband Purshasp returned she told him all that she had learned and together they praised and thanked the Almighty God.

Then the time came that Doghduyah would bear her son. And it was said that during that night the whole city where Purshasp lived became radiantly illuminated: a new, strange, silver-white light shone on the houses, the streets, the trees and the meadows, and was reflected in the lakes and the rivers. And the horse owners and the cattle owners out in the fields or travelling on the roads looked towards the city in great wonder and astonishment. Not until the next morning did they understand that the strange light they had seen, during the night, had been shining from Purshasp's house because of his son being born from the Light which is Endless.

Since the evening before, many people had gathered in the house of Doghduyah and Purshasp, nurses, family and old people. And when the child was born, in the early morning hours when the darkness of the night had just faded away and the first, still hazy, beams of the sun tried to break through, it struck everyone present that the little boy smiled and laughed, while it was a well-known fact that children always cry when coming into this world. And it was the sound of this laugh, together with the radiant beauty of the child which made its father Purshasp realise that his son really was to be a true Prophet of God. He named him Zoroaster, the Blessed One, as had been predicted by the old seer. And there was great happiness in the house of Doghduyah and Purshasp.

The news of Zoroaster's birth quickly spread throughout the city, and the wicked, bad and mean people gathered together to discuss how to find means to kill this little boy before their fear that eventually he would destroy them, came true. And the rumour went further and further until it reached the ears of King Daran Sarun, who ruled the country of Media in those days and who refused to believe in God, but practised magic instead and had his own man-made idols to whom he daily prayed.

During these last months he had already heard several times from astronomers and historians that a boy would be born in the country who would one day be a powerful sovereign, destroying all the wicked people and all magicians and guide the people back to the old, true and only faith in God. And King Daran Sarun was afraid.

And when the news of the circumstances of Zoroaster's birth came to him, the fear in his heart grew and made him hurry to Purshasp's house. He forced himself into the room where the little boy slept peacefully in his cradle. It had all happened so quickly that no one present realised what the king intended to do. But when he put his hand on his sword to cut off the child's head, Doghduyah suddenly screamed in terror, and at that very instant the king's arm and hand became dead; a greyish pallor spread over his face, and he staggered from the house in agonising pain.

When this story went round the city, Zoroaster's enemies, the magicians and bad people, were greatly alarmed, and in their anger and fear, they went to his house, took him by force from his father and carried him off to the desert. There, in a deserted spot, they piled wood and straw together and set it on fire. Then they threw the baby boy on the leaping flames. After satisfying themselves that the fire was burning fiercely, they hurried back to the city to proudly tell their king that Zoroaster was being consumed by fire.

But they had forgotten one thing: the God of Gods rules over fire as well as over people. And He changed the leaping flames into soft pearls of dew in the midst of which Zoroaster slumbered peacefully.

Doghduyah, in great fear for the child's life, went from house to house, asking where her baby was. God sent a message into her heart telling her where she could find her son. She went out into the desert and secretly carried him home.

The magicians and the people of evil spirit were extremely disappointed and angry when, after some days, the news of Zoroaster's survival became known in the country. They again gathered at his house and by order of the king took him away from his parents who were quite helpless being only two against so many.

His enemies brought him outside the city to a narrow passage between steep rocks, knowing that in the evening a large herd of cows would pass, and there they left the helpless little boy on the ground, knowing that he would be trampled by the animals. These heartless people went away and Zoroaster remained there, kicking with his small feet and groping around with his hands, not knowing what terrible fate awaited him. It became evening and the deafening noise of the stampeding herd of cows came close. But oh, wonder, one powerful cow ran ahead, and when she saw the child, she suddenly stopped in her run and slowly came near. She bent her head and softly licked the boy over his face. Then she stood over him so that he was safely shielded between her feet. The cow then angrily used her horns to drive away whichever other cow came in her direction. She stood there, like an immovable rock, and guarded the baby until all of the cows had passed and only then did she join them. And the child fell asleep and it was thus that Doghduyah found him after a fruitless search in the city and its surroundings. Her heart was filled with gratefulness as she, although not having been there, understood that again God had saved her child from a terrible death.

But still the king refused to accept the fact that Zoroaster because of his prophethood was greater than he, and he ordered his servants to go out into the country and find the hiding place of the wolves. Then once they had found it, he ordered them to slaughter all the cubs when the wolves had gone out during the daytime, and take Zoroaster and put him in this cave in the midst of the blood so that the wolves on returning in the evening and seeing the child among their killed cubs, would, in vengeance, throw themselves on him and tear him to pieces. And all was done and arranged according to the king's orders.

Late in the evening the wolves returned to the cave. From afar already they smelled the blood of their cubs and when they approached, they saw them lifeless, slaughtered and bleeding, and they saw the child, alive. Their anger was boundless. Growling they came near, and the chief wolf wanted to throw himself immediately on the child, but the boy, as if by accident, while groping around with his small hands, touched the wolf on the head and at that same moment the miracle took place: the wolf seemed to forget his anger. He became friendly and his angrily-opened mouth closed. The other wolves, seeing the attitude of their chief, did not dare to attack the child. And so they passed the night sitting around Zoroaster and watching over him as if God had appointed them to be the guardians of His Prophet.

And even in the hiding place of the wolves God looked after the daily needs of this child: two sheep came down from the mountainside and they entered the cave without any fear of the wolves. They went to the little boy and he sucked from their milk. After he had drunk and felt satisfied, he fell asleep and the wolves and the sheep slept with him.

In the morning after the wolves had left, God showed Doghduyah where to find her child. Entering the cave she could not believe her eyes, and she did not know how to find words to thank God.

It was after this last failure to kill him that the magicians and the enemies of Zoroaster became despondent. And one day when they all came together to exchange views on the strange, inexplicable events that had passed, a wise old man named Purtarush stood up amongst them, and he spoke, saying:

"I am an old man and I have seen and learned many things. I have studied old scriptures and Holy Books and my advice to you all is that you should stop thinking of ever killing this child. Zoroaster is not to be destroyed by any humanly created plans. The God of Gods is his friend and the Angel Gabriel, the splendour of God, is with him and will always be at his side to save him from danger and shield him from all evil. It was for this reason that the child laughed on being born: he felt secure in God's love."

The old man looked around and raised his voice as if he wanted all living people on Earth to hear and understand his words:

"And I tell you that the time will come that he will be the Guide of all people; his laws consisting of the teachings of God and His commandments will be accepted and followed. Through the ages people will remember his name: Zoroaster, the Blessed One, because through him God will make mankind again understand that His Love and His Light are endless."

Abraham

5

Abraham

It is related that long, long ago the lands around Babylon were ruled by a young and noble king named Nimrud who governed his subjects with justice.

However, when the king became older, the wealth of his country and the splendour in which he lived did not fail to have their influence on him. He saw himself as the creator of all the good things in his kingdom and on the Earth, and consequently wanted the respect and adoration of his subjects for himself alone. Overstepping the dignity of a sovereign, he wished to be considered a God. Idols in his own likeness were erected in every temple throughout the country and the people were forced to worship these images of him. Nimrud, the once noble and just king gradually, as the years went by, changed into a tyrant.

By accepting Nimrud, a human being, as their God, the people were paving the road for jealousy, hatred and greed to grow in their midst. And the few who, secretly, were still following the old teachings, were severely punished when discovered.

And so the time came that God, the Only One, in His great and eternal love and compassion, decided by means of dreams and the formation of the stars, to make it known to the soothsayers and astrologers of the country that during a certain month of the year a child would be born in the village of Kosh near Babylon who would one day abolish the existing idolatry.

One day when Nimrud was sitting in council to decide on certain state affairs, his wise men suddenly approached him in great confusion, saying that the country was in great danger.

They had learned during the past days that in the coming year a man of wonderful power and great authority would be born who would guide the people to a new religion and a new law and do away with the idols; consequently he would cause the downfall of the dynasty of the House of Nimrud. Thus it became known to the world that the God of Gods would send His Prophet.

Nimrud, on hearing these words, flared up in fear and anger and immediately decided on steps to be taken to prevent this event from happening. All male babies were to be given to the king to be killed and soldiers would be appointed to patrol day and night in the streets and around the village of Kosh, searching the houses for baby boys and preventing new marriages. To make certain that for the time being no marriages would take place, a mandate was issued from the court that from that evening onwards all men should leave the village for a certain time and secret watchmen would be stationed everywhere so as not to allow any one to leave or enter Kosh.

The king's orders were carried out at once: the hard, ruthless steps of the soldiers could be heard in every deserted lane; frightened women were crowding together in the houses, not understanding what was happening around them, and those who were pregnant were living in constant fear that their babies would be boys.

On the outskirts of Kosh there lived a young man, Tarukh, who, although his family was related to the royal dynasty, was a God-fearing man into whose house no idol had ever entered. Tarukh was manager of the royal treasury—Minister of Finance—and hence a confidant of the king. For the last few months he had been wanting to get married and he and his fiancée Usha, a sweet and lovely girl from one of the other villages, had been planning when and where their marriage should take place.

Tarukh was again thinking of all this when the orders of the king reached him that he should come at once to court where he heard the news of the latest war-like measures of King Nimrud, and was ordered to stay with the king to advise in what other ways this disaster of a coming prophet could be prevented.

And so daily life continued in Kosh, once a village ruled by joy and beauty; now a place governed by fear, frustration and loneliness.

After a few weeks a special message had to be delivered to someone living quite near Kosh and the king, trusting no one else, sent Tarukh, telling him at the same time that he had been selected to do this, in preference to others, on account of his perfect trustworthiness.

When Tarukh had finished his errand, he decided to spend a little time with his family, as he had not seen them for a long time. On coming home, he discovered that during his absence his fiancée had come to live with his mother. That day, while talking after the evening meal, his mother suggested that he should get married then and there so that his house would be Usha's real home making her peaceful during these frustrating days of separation. After some consideration Tarukh agreed to this and the marriage took place secretly with only a few friends and members of the family. When Tarukh went away after a few days, to go to the court again, he left a grateful and happy wife.

Gradually, as time went by, it appeared that daily affairs in Kosh could only be managed with great difficulty as there were no men to help with them. Thus King Nimrud decided that the time for the men to return home had come, and normal life was assumed soon afterwards. But the orders that all male babies should be given to the court, still stood. It was therefore with mixed feelings that after some time Usha discovered that she was pregnant: a joyful longing for this child and a growing fear for the consequences. For some time she kept her pregnancy a secret from Tarukh, not knowing what his reaction would be as he was a confidant of the king. When it was no longer possible to do so, she decided to go to him and tell him that she was with child and in her fear she suggested that it would be a good thing to tell the king in case it was a male. As the king had always been good to them, perhaps his favours and gifts to them would become even more numerous. Tarukh consented to this advice.

At that time King Nimrud decided on some new tax regulations and in this connection ordered Tarukh to come and live at the court for the time being. During his absence, when Usha felt that her time had come, she went outside the village to the moss-grown velvet bed of a waterless river where in the cool shade of some overhanging trees, she gave birth to a beautiful baby boy. He smiled and it seemed as if all of nature smiled with him. Then she wrapped him in swaddling clothes and looking around for a hiding place for him. Close by she found a spacious cave as if God Himself had prepared a place for His Prophet to hide. She left the baby there and quickly went home. Then she sent word to Tarukh to tell him of the birth of their son who was very sickly and died almost immediately after he was born. Tarukh believed her and was grateful for her own safety.

Shortly afterwards Tarukh returned from the court and their life seemed to assume its old regular pattern. But whenever her husband left the house, Usha used to hurry away to the cave to suckle the child. Once when she could only come back to him after several days, she saw to her great astonishment that the child was happily moving about, sucking milk from one, and honey from another, of his own fingers.

Accordingly the child grew up in this cave, only seeing his mother during the few hours she could spend with him when his father had gone out to work.

Years passed by in that way and the time came when the boy wanted to see more than just the walls of the cave. It must have been evening, that first time when he came out and the world was new to him; a dark sky with a faint light at the horizon where the sun had set. He saw a star and full of joy exclaimed: "This is my Lord," but when it set, he said: "I do not like those that set." He stayed there, outside the cave, sitting on a rock, and when he saw the moon rising he thought: "This is my Lord," but when it also set, he said: "Truly, if my Lord does not help me to find Him I shall certainly become one of those erring people." And when finally he saw the sun rising, he got up and said: "This is my Lord, because this is greater than the stars and the moon," but when after a day's glare it also set he bowed his head and said: "Really I want to stay away from all the things which you, my people, associate with God, I direct my face unto Him who has created the heavens and the earth."

Gradually it became clear to Usha that her son was extremely wise for his age and it is related that one evening when she was again playing with him, he asked her whom she thought their creator to be, to which Usha, afraid that even the walls might listen, replied: "The king." Her son looked at her for a while, then he asked whether the king was more handsome than his father Tarukh. Usha shook her head, then the boy said: "If the king would be my father's creator, why then has he made him more beautiful than himself?"

He got up, took her hand and led her outside the cave where, in the dark night, he showed her the stars, the planets and the moon and explained to her about the greatness of the earth, the height of the skies, the unbounded world and the immeasurable universe.

In astonishment Usha looked at her son whose knowledge was far beyond her comprehension. She saw the beauty of his face, his reassuring smile and his eyes which understood more than she would ever know, and slowly the realisation came to her that she was looking into the face of a child sent by God to become His Prophet. Quietly she got up and left him alone.

When Tarukh returned to the house he saw that she was confused; on asking her she replied that she carried a secret with her which she could not tell, could not reveal and could not conceal. Worried, he pressed her to tell him, on which she answered that the person who was expected to change the religion of the world was his son. And then she explained to him everything about their child having lived in a cave during these last years; how he had grown and the questions he had asked.

Tarukh was very much astonished to hear all this and together with Usha he at once went to the cave where he beheld his son in delight and gratefully took him in his arms. The parents looked at each other over the head of the boy: Usha's face wet with tears and Tarukh with a proud expression in his eyes, and at that moment they understood that they had to give up their son into the care of God. It was then Tarukh's idea to call his name "Abraham" as he would be the leader of many peoples.

Shortly after this Tarukh died suddenly and Usha and her son were left in the care of Tarukh's brother, Azar, who was a great craftsman making idols for King Nimrud and quite famous in this art.

When Abraham was still very young—he must have been five or six years old—his uncle sent him into the streets with a basket full of idols which he had to sell to the people. Instead, the boy started to talk to the people, telling them to leave idolatry and to begin worshipping the Only God Who is merciful and loves His creations with compassion and understanding. Messengers brought the news of a boy, talking at the corners of the streets about the One and Only God, to Nimrud, who ordered Abraham to present himself at the court. There the king, angry that Abraham did not kneel down in front of him, asked him who his creator was. The answer came immediately: "My creator is He Who causes one to live and to die." At once Nimrud ordered two men to be brought from the prison, one of whom he killed, and the other he allowed to depart. Turning towards Abraham the king said: "I have caused one of them to die and the other to live." Abraham replied: "My creator causes the sun to rise in the East; please do likewise in the West." Then Nimrud became confused and Abraham left him.

Within a few days this story became known in the lands around Babylon and gradually more and more people started following this boy, who possessed a wisdom so far beyond his age that only God could have given it to him.

After some time the Festival of Idolatry was proclaimed throughout the country. It was a custom that on this holiday all the people who during the past days had prepared beautiful garments and lovely food, would gather and in a long procession bring them all to the idol-temple to place them in front of Nimrud's stone images. Afterwards they would present these gifts to each other, convinced that the blessings of their idols were with them. All this was considered an act of good omen and hence an occasion for joy and pleasure.

On the day of the festival some people asked Abraham to accompany them, but he refused, pretending to be sick. He stayed home all day, but in the evening when everyone had left the temple to amuse themselves in the streets and houses, he took an axe with him and quietly went to the idol-house, where he smashed all the idols to pieces, except the largest one upon whose neck he hung the axe. Thus the idols were found the next day when the people returned to their temple. They shouted and lamented and prayed to their idols to curse the guilty person.

As it was understood that he was only one person could have done all this, Abraham was summoned to the court where King Nimrud accused him of having committed this crime. Abraham denied it, saying that the biggest idol had done it; then he added: "Why don't you ask them and see whether they can speak." After these words silence hung over the court; people hesitated, not knowing what to say or to do. Then Nimrud, who in front of his subjects had to show courage, said: "But you know that these cannot talk," whereupon Abraham answered: "Then do you worship something which is mute besides God?" There was no answer to this, and seeing Nimrud's confusion, the people went away, leaving their king alone in his rich palace but with an empty and angry heart.

After some days when Nimrud saw that his subjects were favourably inclined towards Abraham, he ordered him to be imprisoned. Then he held counsel with his wise men and it was decided that Abraham should be burned. An enclosure was made at the foot of a mountain near Kosh: sixty cubits long, forty cubits wide and with walls seventy cubits high. Nimrud ordered that, as an obligation to the idols, every man should carry a donkey load of wood into the enclosure. Then the fire was kindled and it was so high that its glow could be seen from everywhere in the country; birds could not fly across the flames and people were not able to approach the walls of the enclosure owing to the immense heat.

A catapult was constructed and Abraham bound hand and foot was put on it. At that moment the angels approached the throne of God, asking Him to allow them to save Abraham. And God answered, saying that they might help him, but that it would be strange if he needed their assistance.

Two angels, in charge of rain and wind, went down and asked Abraham whether they should send a cloud with rain over the fire to extinguish it, but Abraham refused, knowing that God, for Whom he had been born, and to Whom his life was dedicated, would be with him.

When he had been projected from the catapult and was near to falling into the fire, Gabriel met him in the air, asking him whether he needed anything, but again the reply was: "No, not from you."

Then Gabriel advised him to ask help from God, on which Abraham answered: "Inform Him of my case and my safety will be cared for." And God's order came: "Oh fire, be cold and safe unto Abraham."

Angels took hold of Abraham's legs and arms and softly placed him on the ground; Gabriel brought a beautiful garment for him from the Gardener of Paradise; and by the mandate of God, a space of twenty feet long and as many wide opened in the fire. He surrounded Abraham with plants, blossoming flowers and a fountain of delicious cool clean water. An angel was sent down to keep Abraham company and every day food was brought from Paradise.

When eight days had gone by and the fire subsided a little, Nimrud climbed onto the highest building in the neighbourhood and looked over the walls of the enclosure into the fire. To his immense astonishment he saw Abraham sitting with someone else among lovely flowers on a broad green lawn, near a fountain of crystal clear water. This, Nimrud thought, must be Paradise. His failing to understand what he saw, turned into fear and in agony he shouted to Abraham, asking him how he had been saved from the fire. Abraham, hearing his voice, replied that all this had happened by the grace of the God of Gods. Then Nimrud enquired about the person near Abraham and was informed of his being an angel sent by the Almighty to keep him company. The king then asked Abraham to leave the fire and come to him. Abraham got up and the flames gave way, making room for him to pass through until he stood in front of Nimrud, whom he asked to confess the unity of God and to acknowledge the truth of his mission. But Nimrud asked for delay to consult his wise men, and it was their suggestion that the king should challenge Abraham to fight.

Abraham felt disappointed that his king still refused to believe and he agreed to fight. On the appointed day Nimrud marched out with a perfectly organised army which halted in battle array on a spacious plain. Abraham came from the other side and halted, quite alone, opposite Nimrud's army. The latter, amazed, asked Abraham where his army was, on which he received the reply that God would send it. At the same moment countless numbers of gnats appeared. They were everywhere; suddenly; in the air, on the ground, on the soldiers and on their arms, and the whole army, including King Nimrud, was killed, even their flesh and bones were eaten so that no trace was left of them.

Somewhere on the outskirts of the village, Usha silently prayed for the safety of her son whose greatness, although he was still very young, had been obvious after this last battle. A king who could have become a blessing to his people, became a curse and there had been no joy in Abraham's heart when he returned to Kosh. He had conquered but his pity was with the vanquished. When he had quietly withdrawn within the house, the people came out into the streets and they whispered and talked to each other about this boy whom they had seen growing up in their midst and who was to become God's Prophet to lead them to a new religion and to guide them to the Only, All Powerful and Merciful God. A Prophet carrying his name in honour and with dignity: Abraham, Father of Heights, Father of Many Peoples.

Jesus

6

Jesus

Palestine and the Jews; a small country and a small nation on the eastern Mediterranean shore; once righteous and prosperous, but in those days unfaithful to God, stricken with poverty and occupied by the mighty and ruthless Roman Empire. Everywhere and always the people had to submit to rules and regulations set down by a hateful emperor living in his wealthy palaces, far away, in Rome. The Jews suffered and felt deserted: the emperor disinterested in their fate; their appointed governors tried to be friendly with the occupying forces to gain more power and wealth, an attitude which was even followed by many of their priests. And the poor were suffering in silence at the merciless hands of the rich. Mistrust and hate ruled the days, and fear and sorrow the nights.

However, although they did not know it, God, the Lord, the only One, who rules the Universe, the seasons, and the World with all its nations, was with them in their sorrow. He knew that not only did they suffer because of foreign armies marching through their cities and lands, but even more so because of their own failure to keep to the Commandments He had given them long ago. His own words had become lost to them resulting in backbiting, jealousy and sinful behaviour, and in His endless love and mercy, the Lord decided that a Prophet should be born in the country of Palestine; a man, who, by his righteous and faithful behaviour would be an example to them and show them the true path towards the Light.

At that time in Nazareth, after waiting long, a daughter, Mary, was born to a middle-aged couple named Yonakhir and Hannah.

The girl grew up and it was a daily joy to the parents to see her lovingly move about amongst the neighbours, the cattle and in the fields.

When Mary was fourteen years old her parents died. The priest, Zadok, and his wife, Shami, good friends of Mary's parents, took her to their house as though it was an order from God. And Mary was happy until a few years later Shami also died.

On being requested by Zadok, the chief priests then ordered everyone to gather on the next Sabbath to pray and ask the Lord whether Mary, who had attained womanhood, should now be given in marriage or not. Among the gathering people was a carpenter named Joseph. While praying they were astonished to see a snow-white dove suddenly fly out of the sanctuary and alight on the top of Joseph's stick, from where it moved to his head and then returned into the sanctuary. Joseph, recognising the will of the Lord, and grateful for having been appointed to be the husband of this sweet and innocent maiden, got up and took her to his house where he did everything to make her comfortable.

Then the chief priests wished to have a coloured curtain made for the temple by girls who were known to be righteous. Mary was one of them and she spent most of her time weaving in the sanctuary of the temple. High up in the wall there was a window through which golden sunbeams fell down on the colours which moved through her busy hands, and she was content and happy and usually sang while working. Occasionally Zadok came in to see how she was and how the work was progressing, and always he was surprised to see a small basket full of lovely fruits and food standing by her feet. Once he had asked her where this came from and Mary's reply had been: "It is from God, for God supplies whom He will, without reckoning." From when she was a child she had known that all good things come from the Lord and so to her there was nothing astonishing in the fact that God, Who had always looked after her, was daily supplying her with fresh fruits and other food. But the priests talked about it among themselves and were wondering.

One day, when Mary was happily working, there suddenly stood an old man in front of her. She looked up in surprise. Then his greeting came: "Peace be with you; You who are blessed among women; God be with you." While Mary was wondering about the meaning of these words, the man continued: "Fear not, for you have found grace and mercy with the Lord. I have been sent to announce to you that you shall bear a son and call him Jesus. He will be great because he shall be called the Son of the Highest." Mary became very quiet upon hearing these words. And suddenly the old man was no longer old, but his appearance changed and she saw the Angel Gabriel, the Lord's messenger, in all his splendour of pure shining-white garments, and like a song his words came to her: "This shall be a sign to you: your kinswoman, Elisabeth, even though she is in old age, shall bear a son who will be the announcer of the True Light which will come from you to rise upon the world." Then Mary bent her head in astonishment and gratitude, and folding her hands, she replied: "I am the handmaiden of the Lord, let it be according to your word." Then the angel left her and from that day onwards there was a warm and great joy in her heart and it seemed as if a new and strange light was shining from her body.

On completing the curtain, she brought it to the Chief Priests who blessed her, and, as if given special knowledge by the Lord, they told her that her name would be magnified and that she would become a woman blessed among all the families of the earth. And Mary returned to Joseph's house in great joy.

Some time later she went to see her kinswoman, Elisabeth, who was married to Zacharias, and these two elderly people, having been informed by the angel, at once recognised the strange light and the peace that filled the house the moment Mary entered. Elisabeth, kissing Mary, said: "Peace be with you, you who are blessed among women," but Zacharias, with tears in his eyes, kept silent, moving his hands in sudden gestures, but apparently unable to speak. When Mary wondered about this, Elisabeth explained that the Angel Gabriel had appeared to them also to announce the birth of their son, and as she was of old age, her husband had refused to believe him, on which the Angel had told them that Zacharias would be dumb until his son was born as a token that God's words have to be believed.

For three months Mary stayed in their house and together with Elisabeth she glorified the Lord, still not understanding why He had chosen her to be the mother of the One who would bring the Light to the world.

When Mary returned home, the Angel Gabriel appeared to Joseph in his sleep telling him that she was expecting a baby, a child whom the priests, the kings, the prophets and the governors of Israel had been waiting for since the very beginning of time. His name had been predicted in Holy Books to be Immanuel, King of kings and Prince of peace. He, the Light, would teach the Book, the Wisdom and the Law, and he would take it on himself to save the world from sin. Joseph, on waking up, went to Mary with a heart overflowing with joy and gratitude, and together they prayed and thanked God, asking Him to make them worthy of raising this child. From that day onwards Joseph did not leave Mary out of his sight and he looked after her as a servant.

After some time Caesar Augustus ordered that every person was to get himself registered in his own city. So Joseph had to go to Bethlehem and he took Mary with him.

During their journey, Joseph saw that Mary's face was sometimes sad and sometimes radiantly happy. When he asked her the reason she answered with a sad smile that she saw the nation of Israel which, although they were surrounded by the Light, continued to mourn and weep, like a blind man who cannot see the sun; and she saw the foreign nations, although always having moved in the darkness, recognising the Light which shone on them, and they rejoiced, like a blind man whose eyes have been opened to see the light of the sun.

It became evening, the light of the sun turned orange gold, and the shadows of the trees became long. Bethlehem was not far, but Mary wanted to rest as she felt her hour to be near. On passing a cave they decided to enter. They found straw, water, skins and a manger; evidently this place often served as a stable. After Joseph had made Mary comfortable, he went away to bring a woman to be with her. Out on the road he met an old Hebrew woman on her way from Jerusalem to Bethlehem. When he told her that his wife was giving birth, the old woman at once went with him. By the time they arrived at the cave, the sun had set and there was nothing inside to give them light. But on entering, they saw the place radiantly illuminated with a pure white light which shone from the tiny baby boy in Mary's arms. He was wrapped in swaddling clothes and looked around with happy smiling eyes. While they were standing there, wondering at the light and happiness all around them, some shepherds, who had been out in the field and noticed the strange shine from inside the cave, came in and in reverence they knelt around the child, their hands stretched out to this light, this wonder. And all at once the skies were full of angels singing hymns and praising God. It seemed as if the cave had become a church where every being was praising and celebrating the birth of the Prince of Peace. And quietly Joseph and the old woman also knelt down and prayed to thank God.

On that night an exceedingly brilliant star was sent into Persia and showed itself to the Persians lighting up the whole region of the country. The three rulers of Persia seeing this beautiful star, went to their priests asking them what sign this was. And they, also astonished at the fierceness of the light, answered as if in prophecy: "The King of kings is born, the Light of light, and the star has come to inform us concerning his birth, so that we may go to offer him presents and pay him homage."

And the three rulers took three pounds of myrrh and three pounds of gold and three pounds of frankincense; they clothed themselves in their most beautiful garments, with crowns on their heads and treasures in their hands, and they set out on their journey, just simply following the star. The will and power of the Lord travelled with them and so, in a very short time, they reached Jerusalem where they asked to be brought to the newly-born king as they had come to see him. But the people of the city, seeing all this splendour, became afraid and reported their arrival to King Herod who was ruling part of Palestine by consent of the Romans. Herod called the Persians and when they were brought to his palace, he asked them from where they came, why they had come and whom they sought.

They replied that they were seeking the king who was born in Judea as they had seen his beautiful star, which they had followed. And Herod felt a new and great fear enter his heart that there could be a king who had the power to show his birth by sending a new brilliant star into the sky, and he told the Persians to go and seek the king, and once they had found him, they should return to him and tell him so that he also could go and pay homage to him. But in his mind was the evil idea to kill the king while still a child together with the three rulers of Persia.

And the rulers set out on the road again and saw the star going out in front of them until it stopped above the cave; then it changed and became like a pillar of light that reached from the heavens to the earth. They entered the cave and found there Mary, Joseph and the child, laid in a manger. They approached with reverence, paying him homage and putting their offerings at his feet. They saluted Joseph and Mary, who were wondering why three men, with crowns on their heads and clothed in beautiful garments, were kneeling in the dust in front of this child without asking any questions. When asked, the Persians replied that they had seen and followed the star as it was a sign to them that the most important king of all ages had been born. Then Mary took one of the swaddling bands from Jesus and gave it to them, and they took it from her as a most valuable gift.

The moment came that the pillar of light changed into a star again as a sign that the Persian rulers should follow it to return to their own country. And the guidance of the Lord led them away from King Herod so that they would not mention to him where they had found the child. On arrival in their own country, the priests and important people gathered around them with many questions. They told all that had happened to them and showed the swaddling band which Mary gave them. As the Persians were fire worshippers, they cast the band into the fire. On taking it out it was like snow and firmer than before. Then they held it with reverence, understanding that in very truth and beyond all doubt it was a garment of the God of Gods, for the fire of their own God had been unable to consume it and they kept it in great honour.

When Herod understood that the Persians had left the country without telling him where to find Jesus he was filled with rage and sending for his wise men he asked them where he could find this child. On hearing it was in Bethlehem in Judea, he was determined to slay Jesus.

Mary and Joseph took Jesus to the Temple in Jerusalem when he was ten days old, to present him before the Lord and to give offerings on his behalf, according to the Law of Moses. When Mary came to the door of the courtyard of the Temple, the old man Simeon, suddenly seeing and recognising the beautiful strong light which shone around her, went to her and stretching out his hands, asked her to give him the child. He took him in his arms and knew that at that moment he was holding the King of kings whom all the world had been waiting for. Tears ran down the cheeks of the old man when he closed his eyes and prayed: "Oh Lord, let now Your servant depart in peace, according to Your word, for my eyes have seen Your great mercy."

By that time, messengers of King Herod were sent out into the country to locate newly-born children in order to kill them. Then an angel appeared to Joseph and told him to take the child and his mother to Egypt. The next day they took their few belongings and set out on this tiring journey. While travelling through the desert, they heard, with fear in their hearts, the roar of the lions, but when closer, the lions approached them timidly and friendly, guiding them along the right road, and whenever they turned in the direction of the child, they bent their heads. During the journey Mary sat down to rest under a palm, and, looking up, she saw dates at the top of the tree. She called Joseph to get her some, but the tree was too high and he could not reach them. Then, all of a sudden, there was a voice in the air which ordered her to touch the trunk and when she did so, the fresh ripe dates fell at her feet. After some time they began to worry about water as the season was dry and the days tiresome, suddenly they saw a streamlet close to their feet and they could fully quench their thirst. The Lord guided their way and looked after all their needs.

They stayed in Egypt for some time and during their stay they met friendly and helpful people. Then the angel appeared once more to Joseph telling him that they could return to Nazareth.

Jesus grew up like any other little boy, sometimes intently watching his father's busy hands at the carpenter's work-bench, sometimes herding the cattle with some friends, or helping his mother in the household. Once it happened that he was with some young friends playing on the banks of a small river close by. They had made some small fishing pools and were enjoying themselves in modelling all kind of birds and animals out of clay. Jesus had made twelve sparrows, which he put around his fishing pool. However, it was a Sabbath, and a little boy, being the son of an orthodox priest and noticing that they were making clay figures on this resting day, approached in anger, wanting to destroy the figures. But Jesus clapped his hands above his sparrows and suddenly they turned their heads and flew away. And the little boy who had tried to spoil their fun ran off in fright, not understanding what he had seen.

Mary, with feelings of love and gratitude, watched her little boy grow up, remembering every detail and every wonder connected with his birth, from the moment the angel had appeared to her. There were happiness and peace in her own heart; there was the radiantly illuminated cave where the shepherds had come, and the Persian rulers with their presents, while the angels sang hymns in the skies; there was the journey to Egypt with lions guiding their way. There was so much and she remembered it all and kept it quietly in her heart, knowing deep within, as had been predicted, that her son would be great, teaching the Book, the Wisdom and the Law. The King of kings, the Prince of Peace, who had come to take away the sin of the world.

7

Mohammed

In the lands of Arabia, bounded on the south-west by the endless waves of the Red Sea, and on the north-east by the eternal greyish-brown sand of the desert, where during the day the glaring sun burns on a dried-out earth, and during the night the hard ruthless cold desert wind is the master, there lies a town called Mecca. The buildings, the colour and the environment of Mecca do not differ from any other desert town. Yet, to millions of Muslims, Mecca is the most important town in the whole world and every Muslim should try to have been there at least once in his lifetime.

Long, long ago Abraham and his elder son Ishmael came to Mecca to build there "The House of God": the "Ka'ba", which would stand through the ages as an eternal monument in honour of God; a place where all Muslims from all over the world could meet to be one in their faith and to pray to the God of their fathers. And from then onwards the ordinary trading town Mecca was distinguished among other towns, and it became a place of pilgrimage for Muslims. Years and years later it had to be in this town that the Prophet Mohammed would be born.

To be guardian of the Ka'ba was a great honour and so it was a rule that the guardianship was entrusted to a person descended from a noble and faithful family. In the year 550 Abdu'l-Muttalib was guardian of the "House of God" and all his life he found pleasure in performing his duties as well as he could. His son, Abdullah, was often with him and helped him with the work that had to be done in the Ka'ba, and Abdu'l-Muttalib was pleased to see his son grow up in accordance with the teachings of their faith, which was called "Islam".

One day, when Abdullah was 25 years old, he came out of the Ka'ba, together with his father, and they saw a woman sitting outside in the square. Her name was Koteila and she was known to be a wise and learned woman. And when they came nearer they saw that she suddenly paid Abdullah close attention and there seemed to be astonishment in her eyes and her whole attitude expressed wonder. They stopped by her side and asked her reason for being astonished. Then she looked at Abdullah and pointing at his forehead she told them that she had learned from Holy Books that in the lands of Arabia a Prophet would be born, whose father would be recognised because of a golden shine on his forehead. As Abdullah and his father left the Ka'ba, she had all at once seen a strange light glow over his face and at that moment she had realised that Abdullah's son would be the Prophet that all of Arabia was waiting for. Great was Abdullah's surprise, and full of a grateful joy was his heart when he learned in this way that his son would be a Prophet.

Time passed and Abdullah married Amina, a girl of a reputable and well-known family. Their happiness did not last long as he had to leave her shortly after their marriage to go on a trading journey to Syria. When Abdullah left her, he knew that she was expecting a child and he longed for the moment that he would come back to her so as to be with her when the child was born. But it was not given to him to see his son; on his way back from Syria he was taken seriously ill and he died near Medina two months before the birth of the child.

His wife Amina first tried to get used to the fact that her husband was away and she kept herself busy in her household, but when news reached her that he had been taken ill and died on his way back to her, her sorrow was profound and joy seemed to have gone from her life.

Then, one day, when she was sitting silently in her house, thinking of the happy days when Abdullah had still been with her, she suddenly saw her room filled with a wonderful light. Startled she looked up, and saw an angel standing before her. And the angel greeted her and told her that she was to give birth to a Prophet of God. And as if to underline the angel's words, many miracles took place at that moment: there was a strange lightning in the skies from Mecca towards Syria, followed by a heavy earthquake; abundant rains fell down on the most dried-out parts of the desert so that wheats and vegetables could grow again and the famine disappeared.

And the Angel Gabriel again appeared to Amina and told her that she was to call her child "Mohammed", meaning "He who praises God", and he would be blessed by all the inhabitants of the skies and the earth. And after these words, the idols made by mankind all over the world, were to bend their heads in embarrassment and in shame.

And Amina, seeing all that happened around her, bent her head, and in her quiet corner in the house, she prayed and thanked God for this wonder which was to take place in her life.

In the year 570, on August 29th, a Monday, just before the rise of the morning star, the Prophet Mohammed was born.

According to the custom of the Arab gentry living in the towns, the mothers did not nurse their own babies as the air and atmosphere of the dusty towns was unhealthy. It was better to have the children entrusted to a nurse who lived out in the villages; and so it was decided that Mohammed would be given to a nurse called "Halima", meaning "The Gentle One".

It was evening when Halima and her husband arrived at Amina's house to fetch Mohammed. The journey from their village to Mecca had taken all day, and they were both very tired, and their donkey could not even lift its head from sheer exhaustion. But when Halima bent over Mohammed's cradle to lift the child and she saw his bright eyes resting on her, it seemed as if new strength was flowing through her tired body and she exclaimed her wonder to her husband who also felt his tiredness disappear all of a sudden. They wrapped Mohammed in blankets and took him out where the donkey was waiting and the animal lifted its head and seemed eager to carry this child which had a beautiful face and looked around him with happy shining eyes. Halima, with Mohammed in her arms, mounted the donkey and no trace of weariness was left and they started on their return journey with new strength and fresh courage.

After two days' journey they arrived at Halima's own tribe, the Banu Sa'd, where she nursed him and cared for him together with her husband. And slowly it became apparent that the presence of this child had a rare and wonderful influence: there came welfare among this tribe while, before, they had only known poverty; the lands that used to be completely dried out so that the cattle had always looked meagre and underfed, became dark-green with the abundance of fresh and soft grass. And the child Mohammed grew up surrounded by love and respect.

When he was two years old, Halima had to bring him back to his own mother which she did with tears in her eyes and sorrow in her heart as she had grown to love this exceptional sweet and happy child as if he were her own. But Mecca at that time, was stricken with an epidemic and so Amina asked her to resume her charge and take the little boy back to the village. Halima and her husband were very happy that they were allowed to continue looking after Mohammed and he stayed with them until the age of six.

He used to be out in the fields as much as he could and enjoyed the calm atmosphere and the beauty of nature around him.

Then one morning, when he was near the age of six, Mohammed went out with a little friend to take care of the herds of cattle belonging to Halima. Towards noon, the little friend came running back with a white face and frightened voice and told Halima and her husband that Mohammed had been attacked by two men dressed in white, who threw him down on the ground and cut open his breast. Halima, with great fear in her heart, went at once to the place where Mohammed had been left by his little friend. She found him sitting on the top of a hill, very quiet and very thoughtful. Then, when she questioned him, he told her that two men had come who were dressed in glaring white garments and who had thrown him on the ground and opened up his chest. He had not been able to move and they had taken away from his heart a black clod which they at once had thrown away. Then they had closed his breast again and disappeared like two white ghosts. In this way it is clear that the black part which is in every person's heart was taken away from Mohammed, so that only the good could continue to live and grow within him.

Then, in quick succession, many changes took place in the young life of Mohammed:

First, Halima had to bring him back to his mother Amina, who was very happy that from then on she could look after him herself. But after some time she died and the boy was given to his grandfather, Abdu'l-Muttalib, who would take care of him. But Abdu'l-Muttalib was an old man and a few years later he also died, leaving the care of Mohammed to his uncle—his father's brother—Abu Talib.

Abu Talib's family comprised many persons and it was quite a change for Mohammed to get used to so many people around him after the quiet household which first his mother and then his grandfather used to keep.

Abu Talib had succeeded Abdu'l-Muttalib in the guardianship of the Ka'ba, but he also still continued his own business which consisted of trading with the countries of Yemen and Syria.

One day it happened, after all the preparations for a new trading journey to Syria had been made, that Mohammed, seeing the caravan all ready to go, suddenly could not bear the thought of his uncle leaving him. In his mind it seemed that too many loved persons had left him already: his father had gone before he was born; when he was seven years old his mother, and after her, his grandfather had left him. And now his uncle? No, it could not be. And the boy Mohammed turned away his face which was wet with tears. But Abu Talib had seen the tears and he understood all that moved in the boy's heart and so he decided that there would be no separation, but that he could accompany his uncle to Syria.

Close to the plain, burning, empty desert road which leads from Mecca to Syria, was a monastery, where Bahira, a wise and learned monk, spent his days in solitude to study Holy Books. One day he was walking on the roof of the monastery building when suddenly he noticed a strange cloud. It was pure white and had a longish form. And this cloud moved above and along with a small caravan which went North. Then Bahira saw that the caravan stopped under a couple of trees not very far from the monastery and the people started making the necessary preparations to stay there for the night. Once the caravan had arrived under the trees, it seemed to Bahira that the cloud moved away and disappeared, while now the branches of the trees were bending over the small caravan as if to shield the people from the strong burning sunbeams. Bahira could not believe his eyes: without a trace of wind the trees moved according to the movements of the caravan. And then he saw that the shielding was meant for one person only. And the wise monk suddenly understood: if nature was going out of its way to serve one special person

74

among these caravan people, then that person could not be anyone else but the Prophet whose coming had been predicted by all the Holy Books he had read. Excitement burned in Bahira's heart and he quickly went down from the roof and ordered his servants to prepare a good meal; then he sent messengers to the camping caravan people to ask them to come to the monastery.

When the guests had entered the monastery and seated themselves to eat, Bahira paid them all close attention, one by one, but he could not detect that one person whom he had hoped to meet. When he asked them whether absolutely all of them had come, they replied that only a little boy had stayed in the camp as he was too young to come with them. Then Bahira replied that his invitation had also been meant for this little boy and he sent his messenger to fetch Mohammed and bring him to the monastery.

And Bahira saw them come back, the messenger and the boy, and he saw the strange cloud appear again and accompany them above their heads to the monastery. And Bahira knew, and his heart was filled with gratitude that it had been given to him to be among the first who met and recognised Mohammed, the Prophet of God, whose coming had been foretold by Holy Books, and who, for all ages to come, would be called "A Mercy to all the Nations".